SUCCESS
REDEFINED

PURPOSE

CONNECTION

JOY

LARRY KESSLIN

SUCCESS REDEFINED
by Larry Kesslin

Published by

Success Redefined Press

ISBN: 978-0-9886592-2-3 (paper)
ISBN: 978-0-9886592-3-0 (ebook)

Library of Congress Cataloging in Publication Data on file

First Edition

Printed in the United States of America

This book would not be possible without the love and support of my wife, Ilise, our two children, Drew and Noah, along with so many others. To my parents, Ruth & Howard Kesslin, thank you for all your love and support. I feel blessed to know that all my parents want for me is to be happy.

Finally, to Susan Caba, who made this book what it is. Susan and I have been working together for more than 5 years and her ability to make words edible is something I greatly admire. I know that this book wouldn't be half of what it is without her genius. Thank you, thank you, thank you!

CONTENTS

CHAPTER 1

THE AWAKENING

IT WAS FEBRUARY 26, 1993. I was standing in a dark hallway, breathing crisp air tinged with the smell of wood fires. I was looking into a large gym filled with 85 kids having an amazing time together. They were engaged and connected with one another, laughing and joyous, having just spent the last six days learning to ski on the slopes of Aspen, Colorado. They were here with a youth program that brought underprivileged city kids to Aspen to experience what life could be like if they stayed in school and worked hard. They were from New York, Los Angeles, New Orleans, Denver and other cities. I couldn't help noticing how much fun they were having, even though they had just met one another.

By contrast, I was a 29-year-old regional manager for General Electric, one of the world's most prestigious companies. I had the right job, a good degree from a wonderful college. I was living what most people would consider a great life in New York City.

But I felt empty, like my life was lacking in so many ways. I needed more. Two days later, back in New York, I quit my job. I wasn't certain what I would do, but I knew I needed to work for myself in order to achieve the life I was seeking.

I've spent the past 22 years trying to figure out what those kids had that I didn't. I thought financial freedom would give me happiness and peace, so I morphed from a successful corporate executive into a successful entrepreneur. I did achieve financial free-dom—but not the serenity I was seeking.

That metamorphosis began when I traveled to Africa in 2012 and I started to connect the dots of my inner life. A trip to Nicaragua in 2014 helped me crystalize my purpose in life. I look back now and realize those kids in Aspen and the people I met in Africa and Nicaragua had what they *needed*, while I had been pursuing what I *wanted*. Until recently, I hadn't recognized the difference between needing and wanting. It was the creation of a TEDx Talk in early 2014 that got me to dig deep and realize what it is that we truly need: Meaning, purpose, and connection.

Success Redefined is about my journey to a sense of peace, through the pursuit of meaning and purpose, that I never imagined possible.

I've discovered a new definition of success, one that goes beyond making money and acquiring things. It's a definition that measures success in the depth of our relationships rather than the breadth of our bank accounts.

I've come to know that our connections with others, around a shared purpose, is what truly gives us peace and allows us to achieve so much more together than we can alone. This is my story. I hope it will encourage you on your own journey to a life of connection and purpose.

CHAPTER 2

GETTING TO JOY IS A PROCESS

IF I WERE WRITING A TYPICAL self-help book, I would break it down into something like "7 Steps to Finding Joy" or "12 Ways to Find Fulfillment."

I'm not writing that kind of book. I simply want to tell you my story, how I got where I am, and encourage you to find your purpose and connect with people who share it. Your purpose will probably be different than mine, and how you find it and put it into action will quite likely be different, too.

It's taken me 20 years to reach what I consider this stretch of blue sky, where I feel like I am really soaring. At this point, I know *who I am, what I am* and *why I am.* My life hasn't always gone smoothly. I grew up in a family that rode a roller-coaster of financial tumult. It's only been a year since I gained the clarity to see my path—where I've been and where I'm going. And I have no doubt there will be other turns in the road, because this journey is never ending.

Even though I'm seemingly a poster boy for affluence—one who might not know much about struggling for survival—and these days, even the middle class struggles—I get it that seeking "purpose" might seem like a luxury that few can afford. As my story unfolds, I think you'll come to believe as I do: that purpose is anything but a luxury.

There's a reason people since the ancient Greeks have been asking, "Why are we here?" or "What's the meaning of life?" Because, when you can answer those questions—for yourself—it's as though someone turned on a roomful of lights and life becomes so much brighter.

Purpose is as essential to our lives as the air we breathe. Because, through purpose, we connect to people who share our purpose—and that allows us to connect on a purpose-level, not a surface level.

Some thoughts that guided my search

Basic lessons have come to me in the past 20 years. I'm offering them to you in hopes they help guide you on your own journey or search for a life of joyfulness. As a do-er, someone who likes to get things done, I have learned three key lessons:

1. Humans have a deep need to be connected to others. Not connected as in Facebook friends,

not on a surface level—on a purpose level. We are all looking for our "tribe," the people who know us, accept us, love us and, in the closest of connections, share our purpose.

2. In order for do-ers to really connect, having a purpose is a door to un-lock those deep connections. The closer it is to your soul— the closer you can come to understanding your unique reason for being on this planet— the more joy it will bring you. (Here's a clue: If you decide your purpose is to amass wealth, you've already missed my point.)

3. The joy comes from sharing your purpose with others, from connecting with others on a meaningful level. The result of that connectedness in service of a common purpose is great feelings of satisfaction, achievement and joy in life. It's what Abraham Maslow called self-actualization.

Every quest involves obstacles

Here are what, in my mind, are the barriers to achieving joy through purpose.

- *Distorted sense of need:* In the past four or five years, I kept mulling the idea that people in western societies are convinced we need—must have, can't live without—so many things that are really just things we want or desire. We have deluded ourselves into believing that, if only we could fulfill those "needs," we would also find happiness. We are empty, so we shop to fill the void.

- *False intimacy:* We are, technologically, more connected with one another than at any other time in history. And yet, because our connections are largely superficial, we feel more disconnected than ever before.

- *Fear:* Being afraid of losing what we have or not getting what we "need." Fear puts us back into the void of needing, to somehow make ourselves feel more whole and secure. We see fear as a Stop sign, rather than just a yellow light for caution.

- *Negative self-talk:* We reinforce our fears with the things we tell ourselves—that we aren't successful, that we're about to lose everything, that there is nothing to be done to improve the situation, that life isn't fair. Negative self-talk is a way of giving up our power over our

own lives, by blaming other people or circumstances over which we have no control. That
keeps us from finding our purpose, sharing
and connecting around that purpose.

- *Failure to define success:* As a society, we have
  learned to measure success by the size of
  our bank accounts and an inventory of our
  material possessions, rather than in the depth
  of our relationships and our contributions to
  social good. We accept that definition without
  thinking it through for ourselves.

I've been turning these five obstacles over in my
mind continually in the past several years, discussing
them endlessly with dozens of people. Gradually, I
began to see the connections between these issues, to
recognize how they tied together to create barriers to
joyfulness, how they contributed to my over-all sense
of disconnectedness and emptiness.

What I didn't realize was that my focus on finding
solutions to those problems, ways around those
obstacles, had blinded me to a deeper truth.

It was as though I was chipping away at the
Berlin Wall with a pick-axe, thinking that destroying
the wall would free East Germany. But what eventually

freed East Germans was the growth of their own desire for freedom and their willingness to band together and demand it. After that, the Wall practically came down by itself. When I finally stopped focusing on symptoms and obstacles, I came to a wider, truer understanding of what I was seeking.

Journey of giving unlocks the mystery

It was a family trip to Africa in the summer of 2012 that completely changed the focus of my search for solutions—my chipping away at the Wall. I had thought the trip would be, in part, a lesson for our children on giving to others who had so much less than our family. The trip would reinforce my discussions with them about the difference between wants and needs. And it did do that.

But there was something more. The amazing people that we met in Africa taught us—my wife, my daughter, my son and myself—to look beyond the issues of wants and needs, to see a deeper truth. The people we went to "help" had something I couldn't quite grasp.

I had been focusing on the problem of wants being transformed into needs, and on the issue of disconnectedness. Somehow, if we could change those tendencies, I thought, the world would be more joyful.

But I felt there was another truth that I was missing, though I was beginning to have flashes of insight.

At the airport, when we returned home, it came to me.

Your purpose is never fully achieved; it grows and changes. There is no beginning and no end, only the present.

What those Ugandans had was a deep sense of connectedness to one another. It was so powerful you could almost touch it. They shared a purpose, which was very basic—survival. I realized that I needed a purpose as vital as those Ugandans, something that would deeply connect me to others in my personal and business life. For me, it would not be survival— because my family's survival and stability is pretty much assured, or as assured as those things can be in today's world.

But it wasn't until I began working in earnest on a TEDx Talk about the Disconnected/Connected World in late 2013 and early 2014 that my thoughts finally clarified. I kept having conversations about the speech with friends, family, associates and total strangers. They nudged me into a deeper exploration of what it is that people really need.

Pieces of a puzzle that had been floating around in my mind started to fall into place. I was finally able to fully articulate—for myself, and now for you—my purpose in life and how to use my natural talents to pursue it. (Because I believe your purpose is never fully achieved; it grows and changes. There is no beginning and no end, only the present.)

But the purpose, I have come to believe, is only the vehicle on the journey to joy. To really achieve joy, we have to share our purpose with others. It may be a fine distinction, but I think it is the connections we make with others, even more than any purpose, that will light the furnace of joy within us.

CHAPTER 3

CONNECTED BY PURPOSE, ON PURPOSE

The purpose of life is not to be happy.
It is to be useful, to be honorable, to be
compassionate, to have it make some
difference that you have lived and lived well.
—Ralph Waldo Emerson

WHEN I WOKE UP THIS MORNING, sat up, swung my legs over the side of the bed and put my feet on the floor, I knew exactly what kind of day to expect. A *great* day! There might be aggravations, there certainly would be tasks and chores waiting, and my kids would almost certainly bug me about *something*, but I knew that—at the end of the day—I would look back and say that my day had gone exceedingly well.

I can know that virtually every day will go exceedingly well because I've become clear about who I am, what my purpose is and what I need to live comfortably while pursuing my purpose. I share my purpose openly, which helps me connect with others—whether or not their purpose is mine—and those connections deepen the joy I find in life.

As a result, I don't waste my time trying to find fulfillment in an ever-increasing pursuit of status and material goods. Popeye said, "I y'am what I y'am." I would say, "I know who I y'am, and life is good."

To put it succinctly, I find a lot of joy in living this purposeful life.

Now, before you say it, I know I am not sacrificing anything in pursuit of purpose. My life is good, by anyone's standards. I'm living in sunshine, in Southern California. My work is fulfilling and supports my family in plenty of comfort. I am free to arrange my life in any way I want—to work from home, to take the morning or afternoon off for a bike ride or to play tennis. I spend summers in New York with family, and have traveled around the world for extended periods with my wife and children.

The difference between happiness and joy

It's much easier for someone like me to say I'm happy and to pursue further happiness. I don't dispute that. But, while all of those material comforts do contribute to my happiness, none of them are the true source of my joy. On a trip to Africa in 2012 we saw people living in some of the most basic conditions who were happier than I was at the time. So happiness isn't all about financial well-being. Back in my early 30's I used to say that I would rather be poor and happy than rich and miserable. But in the end, I would really rather be rich and happy.

In addition, I believe that happiness and joy are two separate things.

Happiness is a choice we make in life every day. Barry Kauffman wrote *Happiness is a Choice.* I agree 100 percent with that concept. I believe that happiness is about getting our needs met, but I believe that, as a culture, we have started to confuse what we want for what we need. When we say "I need a better job" or "I need a bigger house" or "I need a smarter child," then we believe that our happiness depends on achieving those results. When I started to realize what I truly needed, apart from what I merely wanted, my life changed dramatically. *I became infinitely happier.*

Joy, to me, is something different. It's an internal sense of deep contentment.

The ancient Greeks described it as the culmination of virtue and wisdom, the "good mood of the soul." Joy is a furnace that keeps you warm even when the world is harsh. Interestingly, a lot of the definitions I found described joy as an absence of fear, even in dark situations. I believe that's so true.

Connection around purpose is the fuel of joy

The true source of my joy is that I feel deeply connected—like you, probably, to family and close friends—but also to a community of people united in a common purpose. Some, maybe most of them, I don't even know. But we are connected by our shared purpose in life.

My purpose is bringing together people who have the commitment and fortitude to change the world. For those who know me or if you first meet me, you will realize immediately that I'm a connector. I put people together, to help them achieve their purpose in life. This may sound a little circular—my purpose is to connect people who share a common purpose— but I think you'll come to understand as I describe my journey to this place of joy.

Both parts of the equation—the purpose and the connections—are essential. One or another is not enough. I believe you need both. The combination results in great feelings of satisfaction, achievement and joy. Some identify it as self-actualization.

To me, happiness is waking up each morning and putting my feet on the floor in expectation of another extraordinary day. Otherwise, the other alternative is not very appealing.

CHAPTER 4

MY STORY

The more technologically advanced the human species got, the more isolated they seemed to become, at the same time. It was alarming, how humans could spend entire lifetimes engaged in all kinds of activities, without getting any closer to knowing who they really were, inside.
—Jess C. Scott

I WAS BORN IN QUEENS, THE youngest of three kids in a middle-class Jewish family. From the outside, our family—three kids, Dad working and, eventually, Mom, too—was as "normal" as it gets. But, at least to me, my childhood was anything but placid. How could I have known that "normal" mostly existed on television sitcoms, and that most families have their ups and downs? Mine was no exception.

My father, Howard Kesslin, was the athletic director at Adelphi Academy, a private prep school in New

York City, from 1953 until 1969. My dad is insanely competitive, even now at 84; I couldn't beat him at tennis until he was 69 years old and I'm a pretty good tennis player. His Adelphi basketball teams won three championships.

"Three? Try five," he reminds me, adding that his teams won a record 50 consecutive games over a three-year period, earning them a certain amount of notoriety and publicity.

My father's bible was the classic, *Think and Grow Rich* by Napoleon Hill. He was an entrepreneur and risk-taker. He even says, "I was the first motivational speaker in the family."

Dad was always looking for the opportunity to make a few extra dollars to augment his teacher's salary. In 1958, he hit on the idea of teaching a Driver's Education class after school. At the time, only a few of the private schools and none of the public schools in New York City were offering Driver's Ed. Soon, students from other schools were clamoring to take the class. My father made a deal with Adelphi to accept students from other schools and split the fees with the school. At its peak, the Driver's Ed program was attracting 2,500 students a year.

"I had found the fountain of dollars," he boasted. The classes were popular with students because they could get their driver's licenses at age 17, rather than 18. Parents approved them because their insurance rates were 15 percent lower if their children passed the course.

Eventually, Adelphi decided the program was too lucrative and took it over completely. They made my father Director of Development, meaning, as he says, "I was in charge of getting money from alumni."

Never stop looking

Cut off from one revenue stream, Dad looked around for another means of making extra money. One of his former ball players had a friend who was trading penny stocks.

"What does that mean?" Dad asked him. "I don't know exactly—he buys stock for 1 cent and sells it for 2 cents," the guy answered.

Not exactly sure what he was getting into, my father met with the guy in his Park Avenue apartment. "I'll pay you $100 a week and, if you do good, I'll let you trade."

My dad had no idea what he was talking about, but he took the job anyway. As development director at Adelphi, he didn't have to show up at the school. So he met this guy at his office.

"It was myself and him, in an office with desks for about 15 people. He was just starting out. I had a phone with 16 buttons. The guy says, 'When the phone starts ringing at 9 a.m., you answer and tell me what he says.' So, at 9 a.m., the phone starts ringing with all 16 buttons lighting up. I answer, the guy on the other end says, 'blah, blah, blah' and I tell that to the guy that hired me.

"At the end of the day, he has this chalkboard that he's been keeping track on, and I see at the end of the day that he's made $50,000. We were market makers. I was so exhilarated, it was like a drug high."

This went on for three months. My father was still employed by Adelphi but he was making as much in a month at the brokerage as he would make in six months in the Driver's Ed program—and more than his annual salary at the school.

Eventually, Dad thought, the school would catch on to the fact he wasn't showing up. He decided to quit his position at Adelphi and go full time as a stock trader and market maker. By then, we were living on Long Island. I wasn't quite six years old. We were, as I said, the quintessential middle-class family. But my father's fortunes—and therefore our fortunes, too—were about to turn.

Keep up appearances, at all costs

When I was six, Dad agreed to open an office for his firm in Florida. We moved to a small town, Bay Harbor Island, and I was enrolled in first grade. I loved Florida. I got to swim every day. I think that's where I got my love for the water and sunshine.

But it only lasted a year. "The market turned," my dad said. It was the beginning of a long stretch of bad timing and financial insecurity for our family. At the end of the school year, we moved back north, to New Jersey.

My father bought a big house in Short Hills. His firm had closed, so he went looking for other opportunities. He invested in real estate development in Orange County, New York. But before any houses could be built and sold, OPEC declared an oil embargo. As a result of the oil shortages, the mayor of New York declared that all city police and firefighters—the target buyers for the real estate deal—had to live in the city. The land deal went sour. Dad took a job as an options trader. He was doing fine—until the market took one of the worst downturns in history. Dad's savings were gone.

"I was broke, bankrupt," he remembers. "I had nothing, not a penny in the bank."

The only asset left was the big house in Short Hills. My father had paid cash, so there was no mortgage. When Dad went broke, my parents sold the house and we moved to the other side of town, to a much smaller house.

I was in the sixth grade. We were still in the same school district, but it was like moving from the rich part of town to the poor part. I had the same friends, but they lived five miles away. Life was screwed up.

I was lonely and isolated at school and at home. My parents didn't explain anything. I was mentally into sports at school, but not physically fit enough to compete. I played the trumpet in the marching band. Winters were brutal. And for me, the worst was my Bar Mitzvah.

Bar Mitzvahs then weren't as elaborate as they are now. But everyone had some kind of celebration and my mother wanted to keep up appearances. We couldn't afford much so my Bar Mitzvah was at home with limited family and friends. The next day, my dad left for a job in San Francisco, which didn't pan out either.

Life lessons learned

When my brother was accepted at Stanford University, he scrambled and managed to get scholarships, grants and loans to pay for school. A year or two later, my sister got into the Fashion Institute of Technology. She qualified for a low-interest federal loan, which she didn't need because she also earned a scholarship. My parents took the loan anyway and used it for living expenses, eventually paying it back.

My father never stopped looking for opportunities. He sold real estate tax shelters and investments in the oil and gas industry. He went into business with an old partner in a company that sold credit card-fax machines. He took a salaried job at Shearson Brothers, then hustled selling investments in Section 8 housing and started earning commissions.

Never hesitate to ask for what you want.

You have to remember, this was pre-Internet days; my father sent innumerable postcards and printed newsletters every month to drum up business. He built himself back to the point of buying his own brokerage firm in 1990, and even went back to Adelphi when he was semi-retired and started a kids' summer camp on the Fort Hamilton Army base.

I learned a lot from my father. Some lessons—many of them—served me well. I inherited some of my persistence from him, my ability to keep forging ahead. I learned another lesson, too, one that's very valuable.

Dad never hesitated to ask for what he wanted. When he suggested using the Army base for a summer camp, someone told him, "You can't do that."

"Why not—did you ask somebody?"

"Well, no ..."

"Get me a contact at the base," Dad said. Soon the summer camp was in full swing and proved very popular.

Like I always say, it doesn't hurt to ask.

It's probably true; too, that some of my early focus on attaining success and financial freedom came from my father. It wasn't so much what he said as what I observed. Life was better when there was money. Appearances were important. The "right" house in the "right" neighborhood was an important social marker. When I graduated from college, I made it my goal to earn at least $100,000 a year. I would climb the corporate ladder to the top. The funny thing is, I never made that goal until I jumped off that ladder.

Why am I telling you all of this? Because I want you to know two things about me.

The first is: *I haven't always been able to easily connect with people.* I felt isolated, disconnected and "different" from my peers starting even before adolescence. And second: *I didn't grow up with wealth*—or even, at times, with the assurance that our family had enough money for food.

I know that saying we need to look for purpose— that feeling connected to others in service of something bigger than ourselves—seems easy when my family is well-fed, well-cared for and living in sunshine in California. That's true; it is easier at this stage of my life.

But I've known what it is to feel disconnected, both when I was struggling financially and when I was financially successful. Part of my success is that I did learn to reach out to others and connect. But part of my emptiness, even when I didn't lack money, was a misdirected focus on material success, on fulfilling "needs" that would define me in the eyes of others as a success.

My father's journey shaped my own. Now, looking back, I can also see how his life foreshadowed some of the lessons I've learned in my life. If we're lucky, we pick up where our parents left off learning and don't have to repeat all their mishaps and mistakes. That's what I want for my two children, Drew and Noah, that they start their lives—their emotional lives—ahead of where I was at their age.

CHAPTER 5

TAKING IT TO THE EDGE

There are known unknowns. That is to say, there are things that we know we don't know. But there are also unknown unknowns. There are things we don't know we don't know.
—Former U.S. Defense Secretary Donald Rumsfeld

BY 1993, I HAD GRADUATED from Rutgers University, taken a job at Westinghouse for a while, and then landed at General Electric. I was 29 years old and still just about as lonely and isolated as I'd been in high school, but trying to convince myself otherwise.

To look at me, you'd say I was motivated and happy, maybe even the picture of happiness. I'd just been promoted at G.E. and convinced myself that I was happy. I wasn't even close. I was a walking robot, empty inside.

Yes, there are both things we know we don't know, and things we don't know that we don't even know. I didn't know what I was looking for, but I knew *something* was missing from my life. So I started looking for it.

Luckily for me, I was searching for that something in what was probably one of the richest self-help eras in modern history. I attended seminars, participated in individual and group therapy, began reading what became a long, long list of books on self-actualization, and listened to various self-help tapes on the way to work. Some were good, some were horrible. I consumed a lot of both.

Sometime in late 1992, I signed up for a three-day self-improvement workshop in New Jersey with a big-name motivational guru. Two relevant things happened there.

The first was a visualization exercise. We were asked to relax, visualize our life and, when we were deep into the exercise, to think of the most fear-based, darkest episode of our lives. We were to examine that memory in detail, then melt it down and shoot it into space on a rocket, out of our lives.

When we suppress bad memories or negative emotions, our ability to experience positive feelings shuts down, too.

Despite my chronic internal emptiness, up until then, I had pictured myself as a person who had no hidden dark memories. Which is why the childhood memory that arose in that exercise, graphic in its details, flooded me with unexpected emotion. That memory isn't relevant here—what is relevant is that it unlocked a cavern of fear and shame I had kept deeply suppressed. Through example, I had learned that fear was something to be hidden and denied; shame was another feeling it was best to put out of sight, locked behind a facade of happiness and accomplishment.

Since then, I've come to know that one reason people are numb is that feeling requires experiencing your negative emotions, as well as the positive ones. When we suppress bad memories or negative emotions, our ability to experience positive feelings shuts down, too. My negative feelings were illuminated and aired out through the visualization exercise.

Joy is more than a paycheck

The second important thing that happened was that the woman who had sold me into the seminar suggested I look into a volunteer program that brought underprivileged city kids to Aspen twice a year, for a week of sports and bonding workshops. The organization was looking for volunteers who could ski, for the winter session. I met with the group's leader, passed muster with him and signed on for the weeklong workshop in Colorado.

Those kids, 14 to 17 years old, were so alive! They had something I wanted, though they certainly didn't have much of anything material in their lives. They vibrated. It was a great week, from one Saturday to the next. I couldn't remember ever feeling so much energy around me. In the end I realized that I had what I *wanted*, and felt empty. Those kids just barely had what they *needed* and yet seemed filled with joy. How could that be?

When I got back to work the following Monday, the first call I took was from the woman who had replaced me in my previous position at G.E. She had a lot of questions. All the energy of the previous week evaporated as I listened to her. Suddenly, it hit me: I had been promoted to a job I didn't want.

I thought about my boss's job, and about his boss's job. I didn't want those jobs, either. What did I want? I didn't know, but not this. So I quit that night.

I needed to feel alive more than I needed a paycheck.

In July, still jobless—though that's not how I thought of it; I considered myself to be on the first stage of my entrepreneurial journey—I volunteered again for the Aspen organization. This time, the program was a ropes course, with lots of trust-building exercises as well as skills instruction. There were about 85 kids from all over the country. Again, I felt their boundless energy.

Then we went to *The Edge*.

For the first time in my life, my mind shut off completely to everything except that moment and that place.

The edge of a cliff, that is. The final exercise required me to stand at the cliff with my toes over the edge and a rope tied around my waist. With the other participants anchoring the rope, I was to lean forward as far as I could over the valley below. The idea was terrifying. I was scared as hell.

But I did it—leaned forward, my heart pounding. I felt like I was perpendicular to the cliff, but I was probably only leaning out about 10 degrees. Then an amazing thing happened.

For the first time in my life, my mind shut off completely to everything except that moment and that place. I saw every rock and tree and patch of ground so *distinctly*. Until you experience it, you have no idea what it's like to be in that state. To be attentive to nothing but what you are experiencing *right now*. Without knowing it, I had been searching for that experience of being totally present in the moment.

There is something about it that is freeing—your whole body language changes, people can see it in your face, you feel so much lighter and easier. It's as though the air tingles around you. The only time that matters is *right now*.

I've been cultivating—or maybe the better word is chasing—the ability to be present ever since that moment on the cliff.

It's not an ability that comes naturally to me at all. Because we can hold more than one thought at a time—pay attention to what we are doing, yet have our mind on something else, we do. Technology makes that multi-tasking easier. I'm sure you see it every day, everywhere you go—people texting or telephoning while ostensibly doing something else.

I wish I could say that being present was as easy as flipping a light switch—or leaning out over a canyon while held by a rope, but it's not. Our daily lives have a way of taking over, and mine was no different. My hyper-awareness of the moment was not permanent. But now I was at least aware of the possibility.

CHAPTER 6

WANTS MORPH INTO NEEDS

If you live for having it all,
what you have is never enough.
—Vicki Robin

Are these things really better than the things
I already have? Or am I just trained to be
dissatisfied with what I have now?
—Chuck Palahniuk

SO THERE I WAS, READY to make money using my natural skills and eager for the exhilaration I felt while hanging over the cliff. I was done searching for a job. I was searching for freedom!

Oh, if only it were that easy! But some lessons—maybe most—are learned in little increments. I knew I wanted the freedom to be true to myself. I just didn't realize what, exactly, that meant. I had set off on my journey but didn't realize the road would be twisty in some places, muddy in others and that the occasional bridge would be down. I might have picked that up from my father's experience, but there are some lessons we just have to learn for ourselves.

And here's where I think our world makes it difficult: We need too much. Or we think we do. So we—especially those of us in the developed world—set off down the road to get what we "need." It turns out to be the wrong road, but we don't realize that 'til we're pretty far along. Some of us never realize it at all.

Losing sight of real need

I wasn't any different. I wanted to be a successful entrepreneur, with all the markers that proclaim success—the nice home, a decent car, the "toys" that consume our leisure time. I wanted to be able to fulfill my every need and the needs of my family. If I could do that, the emptiness inside me would also be filled. Or so I thought.

I had no idea who "myself" was.

But I didn't even know what I needed. I don't believe most of what we think we "need" are needs at all. People decide they "need" things when what they're really saying is they "want" that stuff—telephones, cable television, a third car, a second house.

In the meantime, the idea of "being true to myself" surfaced. I was too wrapped up in what I needed—I had no idea who "myself" was, and I'm sure the same thing happens to others.

These two threads are wrapped up together. I'm going to separate them and leave the part about being true to myself until a little later.

I want to concentrate on the idea that maybe we've become confused, as a society, about what we truly need. Because I am absolutely convinced this is at the root of so much unhappiness, emptiness and world-weariness. I believe that the confusion about wants and needs is one of the big five obstacles to finding joy in life.

Until we recognize the difference between what we need and what we want, we can't discover the purpose each of us is uniquely put on this earth to pursue.

Needs become a trap

Most people that I know wake up with a list of things that "need" to happen that day in order for it to be a good day.

When we take things that are truly "wants" and turn them into "needs," our happiness is dependent on obtaining and achieving those things. And the list of our needs goes on and on, depending on our interests.

Think about it. How many times today did you say "I need..."

What? A haircut, a carwash, a new pair of shoes, a better cellphone?

Cable television? Can you imagine life without it, without the dozens of sports channels and game shows and talk shows and movies and dramas? And of course, multiple TVs because no family wants to sit together in the living room and watch the same thing on television. Too many fights, too much compromising over what gets watched. Besides, maybe you don't want to watch a show when it's on, which is another reason you need cable—on-demand programming.

The kids need private music lessons, specialty camps, sophisticated equipment that our parents didn't have until they were adults, if then. Adults need spa vacations and gym memberships to vanquish stress, not to mention a wardrobe that allows us to dress for success.

We need art and furniture for the house and power tools to take care of the yard. We need symphony tickets to impress one set of friends and box seats at the ballgame for real fun with another set.

Dad's earning his MBA at a weekend program offered by the University. Homework is hard once you've been away from it a few years, but he needs the MBA for his next promotion.

What is the difference between a want *and a* need?

Mom is putting in overtime at the law office, where the work load is unending. Thank goodness— 'cuz we need the money to pay for the boat we'll need next year at the lake.

The kids each have their activities, and need to be schlepped around—at least until one of them is old enough to drive. And then we'll need another car for the kid who becomes the extended schlepper for the family.

Suzy wants to take horseback riding lessons (next thing you know, she'll want a horse—she'll *need* a horse!) Tommy is excelling at ice hockey, which will look great when he applies to college. Geez, though, the equipment he needs is expensive.

Keeping up with our needs requires a lot of effort. We can't afford to be patient, we've got a lot to do to maintain our stuff and get more. Because acquiring all that we now need makes so many of us Very Busy, Very Important People. We are also often tired, very tired.

What do we *really* need?

So, what is the difference between a want and a need?

A *want* is something that you can live without, something that will enhance your life. Don't get me wrong, I like a number of modern conveniences, but I clearly understand that they are wants, not needs. *Needs* are those things that if you don't have them, life would not be sustainable.

I'm not saying you have to get rid of every convenience in your life, or give up *all* the extra stuff and activities that are so demanding of your time. I'm just saying you should recognize them for what they are—they are "extras." And when I say *you* ... it really is meant as a collective *we*.

We may have become accustomed to having more, or to having only the best possible versions of those things—a bigger house, gourmet meals. But if you get down to it, all we need to survive are comfortable-enough, or suitable-enough, or good-enough versions of those things, with enough connections to make life meaningful.

> *If we get to the core of who we are as creatures on this planet, what is it that we as humans really need?*
>
> *What is it that we need to survive?*
>
> *If we can identify that list of needs, what is everything else?*

I've been thinking about this concept of "wants" versus "needs" for several years—maybe it's a natural function of having kids! At any rate, it's been one of my goals to teach Drew and Noah the difference between what they need and what they want. I knew I was on the path to success in the winter of 2009, when we were visiting friends in the Catskill Mountains.

The conversation turned a little philosophical. I mentioned that I thought most people confuse the difference between wants and needs. I turned to Noah, who was then 8 years old.

"Noah, what do you need?"

"Food, water and shelter," he said.

"Then what is everything else?"

"They're *wants*," he replied.

"My job as a parent is done," I told my friend. "My son understands the difference between a *want* and a *need* and he can live a happy life."

But I wasn't quite there, yet. I was still focused on what I thought then were the basics.

When I recognized the difference between wants and needs, when I began defining a list of what we truly *need*—that's when I began to "get" that I was looking for something bigger in life. I wasn't quite on target, my thoughts were still somewhat cloudy, but I was beginning to understand that something vital was missing. I needed to know what it was.

Sometime later, I was telling the story about the Catskill Mountains to another friend. She wasn't as impressed with my insight as I was.

----

*To me, self-actualization is **purpose,** a unique reason for being on this earth.*

"You also need love," she reminded me.

I had to agree. Love and deep connections with others are every bit as important as food, shelter and safety. We will starve without food and water, and a lack of shelter will expose us to the elements. Personal safety and air are pretty obvious, but what would life be without love?

But I also have to admit that I didn't fully "get" what my friend was saying. Even as I agreed with the need for love, I didn't fully understand the depth of the need or the variety of love—connection—that feeds our souls.

Purpose *is a unique reason for being on this earth.*

I'm sure most, if not all, of you will be reminded here of the psychologist Abraham Maslow's hierarchy of human needs, first published in 1943 and expanded in his 1954 book, *Motivation and Personality*. Maslow identified the same basic needs—esteem, friendship and love, security and physical needs—as essential to survival. Unless those needs are met, Maslow said, a person won't strive for what he called the secondary needs: self-actualization and transcendence.

Maslow's Hierarchy of Needs

Until very recently, I accepted Maslow's theory. Then I went to Africa and continued my conversations with others along these lines. And now my thinking has changed.

I think it's time to evolve Maslow's Hierarchy of Needs.

CHAPTER 7

PURPOSE,
THE HIDDEN NEED

True happiness ... is not attained through
self-gratification, but through fidelity
to a worthy purpose.
—Helen Keller

You must read, you must persevere, you must
sit up nights, you must inquire, and exert the
utmost power of your mind. If one way does not
lead to the desired meaning, take another;
if obstacles arise, then still another; until,
if your strength holds out, you will find
that clear which at first looked dark.
—Giovanni Boccaccio

THERE WE WERE—MY WIFE Ilise, our daughter
Drew and son Noah, and me—standing in Terminal 8
at Kennedy Airport in New York, sweaty and stinky
(I speak only for myself!) after a 30-hour journey

from our hotel in Nairobi. The trip was, of course, an adventure but also a way for Drew and Noah to do some volunteer work and see life from the perspective of people whose lives are very different from their own. We went for the kids, but little did I know that this trip would change my life forever.

We were in Africa for a month, volunteering with U-TOUCH (www.UTouch.org), a non-profit organization that had opened several technology centers in remote Ugandan villages to provide basic computer training. The trip took us to several of those villages.

We visited a medical clinic with conditions so unimaginable here in the U.S., they made me shiver. At a college for aspiring teachers, students spent evenings studying by candlelight in dormitories that were shockingly dirty and flimsy by Western standards. I couldn't fathom how the would-be teachers could focus on learning. Yet they were grateful for the roof, such as it was, over their heads and the opportunity for an education.

And here I was, buying a new shirt and deodorant because I was uncomfortable with my own smell and stickiness. A question that had been nagging me at a subconscious level during the flight home was still niggling through my brain.

In that moment, I realized that purpose—
especially a shared *purpose—is one
of our primary needs.*

Why did the people we met in Africa seem so alive, so involved and *present* when their lives were clearly not what we in the West would consider abundant? They seemed to have a focus that reminded me of ... something. Whatever it was, it seemed to have the same effect as hanging over the cliff had had on me. Life seemed more intense, more sharply lit.

And then it hit me. Those Africans shared a common purpose. They were knitted together, connected, in pursuit of a sustainable life. They didn't have time to pine for the latest smart phone or worry about upgrading their furniture and cars. Because a comfortable existence—even survival—isn't a given for them, their common purpose was clearly delineated: attaining food, water and shelter, the necessities of life.

In that moment, I realized that purpose—especially a *shared* purpose—is one of our primary needs. In that moment at JFK Airport I realized that I had spent my life chasing success but what I really needed was to be *significant*. I needed purpose almost as fundamentally as I need air, food and water.

Poverty contrasts with joy

I talked to Ilise about her perspective on our trip. She can still hardly put the experience into words, that's how powerful it was. On the one hand, she also felt the warmth and connections between people who—in American terms—had nothing, yet seemed thankful and joyful for what they did have. On the other hand, she was horrified, especially by appalling sanitary conditions that some in Africa accept as normal.

Ilise shared:

Walking down a lane to a Jewish school that happened to be nearby in one of the villages, I would see the kids and their smiles and the innocence and the joy—it was just unexplainable. I asked myself, *what happy drug are these kids taking?*

These kids had nothing—nothing. They were looking at us like we were amazing. But I thought to myself, 'Whoa! *You* are amazing.' They had none of the stuff, none of the trappings that we take for granted. I wanted to tell them, what you have can't be replaced, it can't be tarnished.

In some ways, I didn't want them to come into the modern world. It's almost like when the British came to North America and showed the Indians 'a better way of life,' which it wasn't. It's almost that kind of analogy to me.

But then we went to see the Maasai tribe in a village in Kenya. They were dancing a dance to hunt lions. The kids and adults had flies buzzing all around them, in their eyes and on their faces. They showed us their huts, which they were so proud of, and there were waterbugs all over and they were so dark and claustrophobic, I couldn't wait to get outside.

The trip was this constant mix of emotions for me, because people were so grateful for what they had, but they were living in conditions that would make Americans cringe. It was a beautiful place, even though there was so much poverty.

What really struck me was when we went to some of the schools, and the students were studying in rooms with no lights and no mats—I'm not talking about the lack of *big* creature comforts. So many kids can't afford to go to school, and so many get malaria because they can't afford clean water.

Our son stood in front of an entire group of sponsored students and said, 'My friends and I would do anything to get out of school for a day and you would do anything to *go* to school.'

So it was a very weird place for me. To see street kids with no shoes begging—that broke my heart. But in the villages, where people had family and love and connection, that was breath-taking because it is exactly what so many have lost in this country.

Most in the middle-class and above aren't consumed by finding food, water and shelter, so we don't realize that we are missing something equally as important—purpose, the hidden need. But we know we are missing *something*, so we keep trying to fill that void with stuff. *More and more stuff.* And for me it doesn't work. The void was never filled that way.

Our new friends in Uganda were not only connected to each other, they were connected to the land because they still farmed it every day. They were also deeply connected to their ancestors because that is where all the wisdom lies. In a culture that doesn't have access to the greatest library in the world, the Internet, they still need to get their wisdom from their elders.

We are meaning-making machines

Obviously, I'm not the first person in the world to recognize the need for purpose in life. Greater minds than mine have been exploring the idea since the ancient Greeks.

Philosophers—some religious, some atheists—have been exploring these questions for at least 2,500 years.

- Siddhārtha, founder of Buddhism, said, "Your purpose in life is to find your purpose and give your whole heart and soul to it."

- Harvard Business Review's best-selling article ever, *One More Time*, by Frederick Herzberg—published in 1968—explained that employees are more motivated by a sense of purpose than they are by better pay.

- Victor Frankl, the Holocaust survivor who wrote about his experience in a German concentration camp in *Man's Search for Meaning*, noted that people who lacked a sense of purpose died more quickly in the death camps than those who maintained a belief in a meaning in something greater than themselves.

I'm not looking at this from a philosophical vantage point. I'm just an ordinary individual, as I assume you are, trying to see what's important in a world that offers so many options, so much stimulus, so many things, that we can lose track of what makes life meaningful. I finally realized that having a purpose in life—being part of something greater than myself—is key.

As humans, we are meaning-making machines—we need to feel that we are part of something greater than ourselves.

As you read *Success Redefined*, I assume that you don't have to worry much about the basics of survival. You don't have to worry about *if* you are going to eat; you might be thinking ... or in some cases, worrying about *what* we're going to eat—hamburgers tonight, or spaghetti? Pizza or Chinese? Shelter? Yeah, we've got that covered. Most likely, the kids each have their own bedroom, there's room for guests and there's a room devoted to television. Unlike the villagers we met in Uganda, we can look for the meaning of life from the privileged perspective of the middle class, for whom survival is almost a given.

If we can divert ourselves from multiplying our "needs," if we can realize we simply *want* the latest electronics, rather than *need* them, we can turn our attention to finding our purpose in life. When that happens, we have a much greater chance of experiencing that inner furnace of joy, because we won't be chasing all the accessories and extras that keep us in competition with the Jetsons next door.

As humans, we are meaning-making machines—we need to feel that we are part of something greater than ourselves.

Live longer with purpose

If the prospect of deep satisfaction and joy in your life isn't enough to get you going on a search for purpose, let me tell you that an ever-growing body of research confirms—not suggests, *confirms*—that meaning in life has a ton of physical benefits. Believe it or not, having a purpose greater than yourself seems to affect your levels of immunity and even the health of your blood vessels and genes.

Older people who identified themselves as having a sense of purpose in their lives are 2.4 times less likely to develop Alzheimer's disease or mild cognitive impairment, according to researchers at Rush University Medical Center in Chicago. Other research indicates that basing your life on meaning or purpose gives you a reduced risk of heart attack and stroke, and is associated with increased longevity.

Even more mind-blowing, scientists at UCLA and the University of North Carolina concluded that your state of mind—your happiness—affects your health at the level of your *genes*. Here are their findings, reported in the *Proceedings of the National Academy of Sciences*:

- People whose happiness is derived from getting, having and consuming more stuff— the scientists called it "hedonic" well-being— showed negative effects. They exhibited high levels of inflammation, and low anti-viral and antibody gene expression (I'm not going to even try to define gene expression. It's a scientific term.)

- Research subjects who stated their happiness came from a *deep sense of purpose* and meaning in life showed exactly the opposite effects. They had low levels of inflammation and high levels of anti-viral and antibody gene expression.

- And here's the most amazing thing. The people who were more focused on consuming felt just as happy as the people whose happiness was based on having a purpose greater than themselves. *But*, at the level of their genes, the more self-centered people had negative physical responses while those whose lives were based on purpose had healthier physical responses.

"What this study tells us," said one of the chief researchers, "is that doing good and feeling good have very different effects on the human genome, even though they generate similar levels of positive emotion."

Let's redraw Maslow's Pyramid

I believe we can start sooner rather than later in life, because when our physical needs are dialed back to a realistic level, we can begin pursuing what is really meaningful. Our individual purpose, the thing (for want of a better word) that makes us unique on this earth. Finding and striving toward that purpose is every bit as important—okay, maybe just a hair less important—than air, food and water.

For decades, our needs as humans have been represented on a pyramid, or Maslow's Hierarchy of

Needs. In that pyramid, food, water and shelter form the base; friends, family and community come after those other needs are met, and self-esteem, recognition and mastery, are one level below the top of the pyramid. What Maslow calls self-actualization is at the peak, to be pursued only after all the other needs are met.

Maslow refers to self-actualization—which I call "purpose"—as an "aspirational need," something that would be nice to attain, but not essential to life.

When Maslow was alive 99% of the population was still in survival mode. In doing research for this book I talked with about a dozen people who have studied Maslow's work, and I now believe that Maslow knew that survival is not only our greatest human instinct, it's also our greatest human purpose. So, the base of Maslow's hierarchy is purpose masked as survival. Maslow knew we needed purpose to connect with others deeply, which I witnessed so clearly in Uganda and more recently in Nicaragua and even on the islands off of Greece.

Fast forward 75 years and survival is no longer an issue for billions of people on this planet. Not only is survival not an issue, we are no longer connected to the land because most of us don't farm it, our food is delivered to our doorsteps. Finally, we are no longer connected to the wisdom of our ancestors because we use Google to find all our information and our elders move to retirement communities to spend time with each other. This is not what I witnessed in Uganda.

In the end I believe that purpose needs to be the foundation of our lives and in a world where survival is a given for the middle class and above, purpose is the most important need—or our hidden need. In cultures that still struggle with survival issues I believe Maslow's Hierarchy is still totally relevant.

The closer your purpose is to your own soul, the more deeply committed you are to your purpose, the deeper your joy becomes.

For cultures where survival is a given, I believe that:

- we need to find our own individual purpose;

- the foundation of our lives needs to be purpose;

- the basic needs of food, water, shelter, safety, love, air and health would sit on a foundation of purpose and meaning.

In other words, we need purpose just as vitally when we're struggling for survival—in fact, when we are struggling for survival, that is our purpose—as we do when we have those basics covered. Purpose must be unhidden and make it a *recognized* need.

My amended image of Maslow's Hierarchy of Needs, arranged as a puzzle with the foundational piece of purpose and meaning. That purpose is our own self-actualization, not our instinctual purpose of survival.

In redesigning Maslow's Hierarchy of Needs, self-actualization was emphasized as a peak to climb to-ward; my Purpose & Meaning model starts with purpose and meaning as the foundational base and then horizontally connects the survival needs of food, water, shelter, safety, love, air and health.

Maslow's Hierarchy Evolved

A least 30 of my 50 plus years has been spent determining my purpose. Maybe, that's a realistic time frame. Finding your true purpose is probably a process, once you stop concentrating on fulfilling those "needs" that consume so much time, energy and attention. I do believe the process will move more quickly the sooner we shake ourselves free of the culture of more, more, more.

I believe that the closer your purpose is to your own soul, the more deeply committed you are to your purpose, the deeper your joy becomes. I'm more "me," more connected with myself, now that I know my purpose on Earth. Depending on your spiritual or philosophical leanings, knowing your purpose may even be the basis of your religion or your answer to the question of the meaning of life.

I'm not here to answer, or even attempt to answer, deep questions about the meaning of life. I'm here to tap into the conversation—and to stimulate it—about how those of us who are privileged; who don't have to struggle for survival, can meet that core need for purpose in our lives.

CHAPTER 8

THE CONNECTEDNESS CONTINUUM

Only connect!
—E.M. Forster

We cannot live only for ourselves. A thousand fibers connect us with our fellow men; and among those fibers, as sympathetic threads, our actions run as causes, and they come back to us as effects.
—Herman Melville

con·nect·ed: *united, joined or linked; joined logically; linked in shared purpose or emotion; to be in harmony with another; having social, professional, intellectual or spiritual values in common; having the ability to communicate on a meaningful level about something important.*

HUMAN BEINGS ARE DEEPLY NOURISHED by their connections with others. Great works of literature, drama, philosophy, religion and now even science all recognize that community—a web of connections—is essential for our well-being. The more connections people have, the less likely they are to be depressed, stressed, ill or lonely. They even live longer.

No two connections are the same. Some are strong and intense, others more casual. Some are just the background colors of your life—the dry cleaner you see once a week or the bus driver who greets you every morning. Even those are important in the overall scheme of things.

For convenience, I've defined five fundamental levels of connectedness in the average person's life. I call that spectrum of human relationships the Connectedness Continuum.

Surface Level
- People you know by name, and not much else
- Social Media platforms: FaceBook, LinkedIn, Instagram, Twitter, etc.

Community
- People with whom you share interests, such as music and sports

Relationships
- One-to-one relationships on any level, such as family members, friends and co-workers

Self

- Connection to one's self

Purpose/Spirit

- Connection to your reason for being

The Connectedness Continuum

I chose the word "continuum" carefully. Connect-edness is not like a layer cake, with sharp divisions between the layers. If you're like most, you have some deep connections that will always be deep and some that are superficial and will never grow deeper. There are others that will either deepen over time, or fade away. And some will fluctuate, depending on what is happening in your life and the lives of your connections.

The most important levels of connection—and maybe the most difficult to get to—are your connection with yourself and connections to others with whom you have a shared purpose in life. Purpose is the key ingredient in both.

The chemical symbol for water is H_2O. Pull apart the hydrogen molecules and the oxygen molecule and you no longer have water. Yes, hydrogen and oxygen are useful substances, but they aren't water. They aren't wet. They don't flow. You can't drink them. You can't swim in them. They are not water.

It's the same thing with purpose and connectedness. Together they form a molecule of joy. One strengthens and enriches the other. They have to be melded—apart, they are not the same thing. Only when paired do they create a molecule.

We could argue about which one is dominant and, in fact, I argued in the past that purpose was the key ingredient. My thinking has changed. I now see that connections with others is important above all else, though I still believe shared purpose is the ingredient that intensifies connections between people.

Adding purpose to your connections with others is like adding a secret spice to a pot of soup. Alone, the soup is nourishing. By itself, the spice has flavor, but nothing to carry it. Adding the spice to the soup raises it from tasty and filling to irresistibly delicious.

All humans crave the feeling of being loved and needed. When we connect with others who share our purpose, we have found the magic combination of ingredients that intensifies the joy we can find in life.

The most important levels of connection— and maybe the most difficult to get to— are your connection with yourself and connections to others with whom you have a shared purpose in life.

CHAPTER 9

FACEBOOK FRIENDS & FALSE INTIMACY

What should young people do with their lives today? Many things, obviously. But the most daring thing is to create stable communities in which the terrible disease of loneliness can be cured.
—Kurt Vonnegut

WE ARE, TECHNOLOGICALLY, MORE CONNECTED with one another than at any other time in history. We wake up in the morning to check our email, to look at our text messages and to be digitally connected to the world around us. We count our followers on Pinterest and Instagram, our friends on Facebook and our connections on LinkedIn. We blog, we chat and we Tweet.

In the end, are we really connected at all?

How many of those connections could we call on in an emergency? How many would lend you $100 if you asked? How many have you actually met face-to-face? How many ... really, how many?

False intimacy is one of the over-arching obstacles to finding purpose, connectedness and joy in our lives. It's the third strand in the spider web spun from wanting more than we need and defining our lives in terms that others dictate—meaning we have to participate in the "right" activities and pursue the "right" goals in life.

The result is we're so busy we have to update and coordinate our online calendars at least once a day, just to schedule a weekly dinner together. We have to check in with our "friends" to see what they're up to, and post our own activities to prove our lives are properly full.

And yet, because our connections are largely superficial, we feel more disconnected than ever before.

Disconnected, Connected World

My grandparents lived in communities that were lacking in "things" but they had something that we long for today. They had connectedness. They lived in communities where grandparents and neighbors helped each other. They held one another's hands when there was trouble—or joy—and they took care of those less fortunate. When someone had need for a babysitter, they called a helpful neighbor or relative who would provide a favor. The "debt" would be gladly repaid in the future.

Technology to displace many day-to-day activities or chores that gave us real face time with other people.

Now we live in beautiful homes in communities that don't even have sidewalks. Many of us have so much wealth that we pay people to provide the favors we used to trade with friends—nannies, pet-sitters, tutors and cleaning services.

Technology opens up the world to millions of people and makes life easier in so many ways. We're so fortunate to be able to stay connected with distant relatives using FaceTime, Skype and other technologies. How many of you remember when a three-minute long-distance phone call was considered extravagant?

But we've also allowed technology to displace many day-to-day activities or chores that gave us *real* face time with other people. When was the last time a group of your friends and family got together to make music, rather than everyone listening individually through their headphones? Our viewing options are so numerous, we don't even have to go to the movies together, let alone sit in one room and watch the same programs together.

If we are meaning-making machines, let's not forget that there is great meaning in day-to-day human interactions. Let's not let technology keep us hyper-connected in ways that allow us to quantify our friends and connections like a ticket taker at a football game.

We don't need to be—we can't be—connected to everyone in our lives at the same emotional level. We do live on a Connectedness Continuum. But I think we can at least try to make every connection authentic on a human level, rather than built on false intimacy.

Know yourself to know others

The most important connection you can make is with yourself. *Not* so that you can remain focused on yourself—*not* so that you can go about your daily life absorbed in your own interests or purpose. *Not*, in other words, so that you can live a self-centered life, basking in your own importance and dedication to purpose. Where it's an all about "Me" world ... a world that narcissism thrives in. That would be just another distorted form of success.

No, the reason to know yourself is to forge deeper connections with others—others who may not share your purpose or be like you or even know themselves very well. The Dalai Lama is a connector. He certainly knows himself and his purpose. And that knowledge allows him to go through life connecting with people, guiding them toward joy without ever mentioning his own purpose. He simply lives it.

Obviously, the Dali Llama has reached a stage of self-knowledge, purpose and being present in the moment that will elude the rest of us. He embodies his purpose so thoroughly that talking about it is just ... just silly. It's almost like talking about what makes LeBron James a great basketball player. He's been at it so long; he's honed his skills so completely, that for him to think about the basics when he's at the free throw line would be awkward. For him, it's muscle memory, embedded in his very fabric as a human.

Connecting on Purpose

Many of the rest of us, though, are still learning ... our muscle memory doesn't automatically kick in.

In my mind, there are people—and I'm one of them—who are driven to "succeed" by doing. We're competitive, we want to win, and we tend to want to "measure" our success by some standard. I'm not saying it's a good characteristic, but it exists.

Embracing and knowing our purpose and values facilitates what I call the "do-er's" ability to make connections. We can align with others around the shared purpose. Knowing that another person shares our beliefs and values helps us build trust in the connection, and to connect more deeply. Without that knowledge, we have a harder time getting into alignment with another, or we may have a tendency to fall out of alignment. It's the way our personalities work. Shared purpose is our vehicle for connection.

Our most important human need is to connect with others and build communities.

There are other people, like the Dalai Lama, who just connect to people naturally. They don't need a shared common purpose; they just connect to the humanity of others. A purpose or shared purpose adds richness and intensity to their lives but they don't need that as a vehicle for their connections. They are all about the connection, and the purpose can be secondary.

Maybe the *do-ers*, myself included, are less evolved. I don't know. We can strive to just "be," but until we reach that level, I think it's fine—more than fine—to connect with others through purpose. For us, it is important to seek and define our purpose, then share it with others.

You may have heard of the phrase that is used to set up a joke, "How do you get to Carnegie Hall? The answer usually comes back in a variation of: Practice, Practice, Practice!

Our most important human need is to connect with others and build communities. Those connections are ultimately what bring joy into our lives. Without them, we feel a void—which we try to fill with other measures of "success." But no amount of money, prestigious memberships or valuable belongings will fill that void.

When we recognize our need for connections and *put our purpose into practice*, we will connect with others heart-to-heart—on a purpose level, not a surface level. The result will be an ever-growing source of great joy and fulfillment.

CHAPTER 10

FEAR IS THE BIGGEST HURDLE

*There are two basic motivating forces: fear and love.
When we are afraid, we pull back from life. When
we are in love, we open to all that life has to offer
with passion, excitement, and acceptance ...
Evolution and all hopes for a better world rest
in the fearlessness and open-hearted vision
of people who embrace life.*
—John Lennon

*Expose yourself to your deepest fear; after that,
fear has no power, and the fear of freedom
shrinks and vanishes. You are free.*
—Jim Morrison

ON SEPT. 11, 2001, I was in the midst of moving.
Literally. I was moving a sofa from our old two-bed-
room apartment in Riverdale, NY, to a four-bedroom,
two-bathroom unit in the same building. We had a

16-month old daughter and Ilise was 8 months pregnant with our son.

The new apartment was more than we could afford but I was confident we'd find a way to make the payments. Closing was scheduled for the following day. And then life changed. Not only for my family, but for every family in this country and for many around the world.

The phone rang at 8:34 a.m. I answered to hear a friend screaming that someone had flown a jet into the World Trade Center. I scrambled to find the television, which had already been packed. I dug up a small black and white television, set it on a box and plugged it in. I spent the next 14 hours glued to the screen. I watched in shock as the second plane crashed into Tower 2, and ash and smoke and debris filled the sky, then rained onto the streets.

I have never been so deeply afraid, not only for the events of the day but for what the long-term effects would be on my life and the life of my family. I had just turned 38 years old, I was about to bring a second child into the world and I had committed to buying an apartment we really couldn't afford. My business was dependent on our clients' willingness—and my own—to fly commercial jets. The nation's airports were closed. Everything seemed to have gone to hell in a hand-basket. What was I going to do?

FEAR = False Events Appearing Real.

Life was suddenly not as sunny as it had appeared just one day earlier. I knew the world was irrevocably changed and I didn't know what that would mean—for the world, as well as for me and my family. I spent many of the next few weeks deeply worried about the future.

And then one day, I found myself on my bicycle at the corner of 125th Street, on the Hudson River, on a pier by the Fairway grocery store. I was looking down the river, watching the smoke that still billowed from Ground Zero. As I looked at the smoke besmirching the skyline, I had a moment of sudden clarity.

Even if I lost everything—my business, our apartment, our savings—I would be fine. My family and I wouldn't be homeless. We had family who would take us in. We wouldn't go hungry. It hadn't been so long since I quit my job and built a successful business from nothing. I had skills. I could do it again.

At that moment, my fear vaporized. And my relationship to fear changed forever.

I had been listening to motivational tapes for almost two decades by that point. One of them—I think it was by Dennis Waitley, a motivational speaker and expert on success—defined fear as False Events Appearing Real (FEAR). In other words, we worry—fear—events that are, in reality, unlikely to happen. We exaggerate risks from catastrophic events, ironically while underestimating the danger from more likely risks. How much more likely was it that I would be injured in a car accident than being killed in an act of terrorism?

Human beings are what I call "meaning-making" machines.

I had intellectually embraced this definition of fear for years, but I never really internalized it until the fall of 2001. The events of 9/11 truly changed my relationship to fear for good. I remembered a saying printed on a refrigerator magnet:

What would you do if you weren't afraid?

So much of what we do in life is motivated by fear, fear of what might happen. And yet, so little of what we fear actually does happen. Until you deal with your fears, you will never be the person you wish to be or were meant to be. I do find it interesting that musicians John Lennon and Jim Morrison—poet-philosophers of our time—articulated so clearly the power that fear holds over us, and yet how easily we can dismiss that fear if we face it.

Reinforcing fear with self-talk

What keeps us from facing fear? Self-talk, that's what. Negative self-talk is tightly entwined with our reaction to fear.

Self-talk consist of the things we tell ourselves that either create or reinforce some belief or value. Self-talk influences how we behave and the decisions we make. Self-talk can be positive: I am a worthy person. But it can also be negative, reinforcing our fears or our false beliefs.

Negative self-talk is a way of giving up our power over our own lives.

Human beings are what I call "meaning-making" machines. Any five people can take the exact same circumstances, define them, and the result will most likely be five different meanings.

Here's an example: Two men fall off the top of a 20-story building. Death is the obvious outcome. One of the men is screaming and crying, the other is laughing.

"What are you laughing at?" the first yelled to the second.

"I'm laughing because I'm flying."

"You fool! You're not flying, you're falling. You're about to die."

"Well, as long as the outcome is the same, I'd rather be flying," said the second man.

Clearly, he was defining the event differently than his colleague. Agree with him or not, he chose a different meaning for his fate. Rather than live his last moments in fear, he decided to die with joy.

We reinforce our fears with the things we tell ourselves:

> *we aren't successful;*

> *we're about to lose everything;*

> *there is nothing to be done to improve the situation; and*

> *life isn't fair.*

Negative self-talk is a way of giving up our power over our own lives, by blaming other people or circumstances over which we have no control.

I'm not one of those people who believe that, if we just tell the universe what we want, the universe will give it to us. I face difficulties head on. But I tend toward the positive meaning of any event. Some people might go to impoverished parts of the world and see only filth and poverty. By looking from a different perspective—seeing the connectedness in the struggle to make a better life—I not only gave the scene a different meaning, I learned how to make my own life better.

Fear is not a STOP sign

We're conscious of some self-talk, but some is a continual, unspoken loop that plays in the background without our awareness. Think of it as a melody with a regular beat—when you hear it, you can't help walking to its rhythm.

Those of you old enough to remember vinyl records were the norm decades ago—interesting, they've enjoyed a surge in sales beginning in 2014 once again. For many, the art work on the albums alone became coveted posters. Within the grooves on each vinyl was the magic—when the needle was lowered, music burst forth. It was ultra-simple. If you scratched the record or let it warp, the music became distorted and the record was ruined.

---

*The ear worm of your self-talk
becomes an obstacle to clarity.*

Our brains are like a vinyl record. They come with some tunes, some grooves, embedded. Some areas are blank, waiting for the music to be inscribed, a process that starts at birth.

Here's the difference between our brains and vinyl: If we scratch the record that is our brain—or don't like one of the tracks—we can use self-talk to create a new groove, erase the scratch or change the tune. I'm not saying it's easy but research has proven it can be done.

Self-talk, or the grooves worn into our brains, become an obstacle to finding purpose and experiencing joy when we pick up a negative "ear worm." You know, when a song or part of one gets stuck in your head and repeats and repeats and repeats...

The ear worm of your self-talk becomes an obstacle to clarity when it's say-ing, "I *need* ..." or "If only I had ..." or "I *should* be better..." or "She would care more about me if ..." Those earworms keep us from acknowledging our purpose in life, sharing it and taking action to fulfill it.

With enough practice, self-talk can change the grooves in your brain to create new, positive beliefs and behavior, or overcome entrenched negative "soundtracks."

Until I faced my fears and realized they were unlikely to come true—but that I could overcome the results, even if my fears materialized—I couldn't move forward freely. I learned to stifle the negative self-talk that reinforced my fearfulness. One of my new mantras is, "Fear is not a STOP sign."

Now, even when I am afraid, I don't automatically define the situation as dire or hopeless. I can move forward and take action. As John Wayne said, "Courage is being scared to death ... and saddling up anyway."

CHAPTER 11

FAILURE TO
DEFINE SUCCESS

*Don't aim at success—the more you aim at it and
make it a target, the more you are going to miss it.
For success, like happiness, cannot be pursued; it
must ensue, and it only does so as the unintended
side-effect of one's personal dedication to a cause
greater than oneself or as the by-product of one's
surrender to a person other than oneself ... I want
you to listen to what your conscience commands you
to do and go on to carry it out to the best of your
knowledge. Then you will live to see that, in the long
run—in the long run, I say—success will follow you
precisely because you had forgotten to think of it.*
—Victor Frankl

I TOLD YOU THE FIRST obstacle is the failure to
recognize the difference between what you want and
what you need. Early on in this journey, I thought that
issue was the whole problem. In fact, I thought this
book would be called *When Wants Become Needs.*

Achieving clarity is a process.

Then I decided the real problem was that we connect on a superficial level. I renamed the book *The Disconnected, Connected World*. My friends would be rich if they had $50 for every time in the last three years that I've said, " I have more clarity now than I've ever had—I am so clear about the theme of this book."

My third—and final—name for the book became *Success Redefined*. Obviously, my thoughts evolved yet again—and I probably owe my friends another $50!

Here's the golden nugget: Achieving clarity is a process. Insight takes time to develop. There are obstacles to making progress. And you can't overcome those obstacles until you recognize them.

But each name, and the process of working through the obstacle it represents, *did* bring me more clarity. And I still believe that one of the biggest obstacles we face in our goal of building community and achieving joy is our failure to define success in our own terms. We think we know what the word means but, when we get down to articulating the definition, it turns out our understanding is either fuzzy or just wrong.

I've come to realize that the way to be "successful" *and* joyful is to redefine success to encompass the spiritual and emotional rewards of life, rather than just the material rewards.

What is your destination?

Those who know me have heard me say this often: If you don't know where you are going, any road will get you there.

If you're on the road, but don't have a particular destination, it doesn't make any difference whether you turn left or right at the intersection, does it? How can you map a plan or a strategy to get where you're going, if you don't know where you want to end up?

One lesson I learned early in life is that having goals is incredibly important. Writing them down and speaking them in public makes them even more powerful. The simpler and more direct, the better. I also bought into the accepted idea that success could be measured in terms of money and things that make life comfortable. Being goal-oriented, I came up with a very succinct definition of success:

Success is the ability to do whatever I want, whenever I want to do it!

Every time I needed to make a big decision, I would return to my definition and make the decision that would lead to success in those terms. The definition was also a guide for setting priorities. That kept me from making impulsive decisions that might have seemed right in the moment, but didn't ultimately lead to my desired destination. So I started my quest.

I was putting together a very difficult puzzle, one with an abstract image and not a lot of clues to the final picture. The top to my puzzle box had disappeared! I'd gotten a big corner section done when I realized I wanted to start my own business. Discovering that it wasn't a corner section after all, just a part of the middle. I fiddled and fiddled with the pieces, but couldn't make any sense of their overall meaning. Some sections escaped me for the longest time.

A good example is how long it took me to realize that I couldn't make someone else happy.

In my late twenties, I was dating a woman who lived in Dallas. I moved her to New York so we could live together. Three weeks after she moved in, I knew we'd made a mistake. And I told her. But we continued to live together for another two years. Get this. It was the woman, not me, who eventually left our relationship.

I was being the person I thought she needed me to be. I was trying to save her—from what, I'm not sure. There were two problems with that. A: She didn't want to be saved and B: I hadn't yet learned that you can't save anybody, you can't make anyone else happy.

The reason that trying to "save" my girlfriend was an obstacle to finding my purpose—wasn't anything about her. The problem was that I wasn't being true to myself. She just wanted me to be me. I was so busy trying to please her, I couldn't find myself. Probably, that's why she had the good sense to leave. Now I know that happiness is up to each individual. We can empathize with the problems of others, but we don't have to solve them.

I wish I could say I came to those realizations immediately after the end of that relationship. I didn't. It took another twenty-some years before the light dawned and I saw where that part of the puzzle made sense. Once I recognized what I had been doing, I could be true to myself. That's what I mean by progress being gradual.

Let your definition evolve

Back to the meaning of success. Eventually (and not all that long ago), I came to the realization that I *could* do whatever I wanted, whenever I wanted— only I still felt a bit empty.

I decided that overcoming materialism—or at least recognizing it—would solve the problem. I talked a lot about how Hollywood, Madison Avenue and Wall Street had imprinted "need, need, need" on our brains and warped our values. Then I decided that superficial connections, combined with materialism, were at the root of the problem.

Well, you've heard the long version of the story. I was still searching for that vague "something" that would really light up my life. My destination—a fulfilling life—remained the same, but I began exploring the intersections of success, purpose and meaning as the path to reaching that goal.

As I shared earlier, I think there are two kinds of people in the world—the *do-ers* and the *be-ers*. My wife and a few other people I know are be-ers. Ilise doesn't really need a shared common purpose to connect with people. She's basically a huge human heart, connecting with people deeply regardless of their purpose or hers. On the other hand, my do-er side leads me to be more competitive, needing goals, and requiring some way to gauge whether or why I should connect with another person. I may aspire to be more like Ilise but I'm comfortable with the reality that I need something more concrete on which to build relationships.

For do-ers like me—and I believe a lot of successful entrepreneurs are do-ers—I think a good place to start is to re-examine the definition of success. Being clear on definitions helps me get clear on priorities. And having priorities means deciding what to eliminate from life as much as focusing on the activities and values to include.

When I start to work with clients, one of the first things I do is give them a list of terms that relate in some way to the concept of success. I ask them to think about the meaning of the words in their own lives. Here's the list, with my own definitions. What are yours?

My Definitions: What are Yours?

Money: A tool that allows us to obtain what we need and want, and help others extend their lives beyond survival mode.

Achievement: Working hard toward, and reaching a desired outcome.

Happiness: A choice to be happy when I wake up and my feet hit the floor.

Joy: Connecting deeply with others, especially those with a shared purpose.

Work: I don't go to work, I wake up each morning and just exist and do what comes naturally, and some of it creates income.

Needs: Food, water, shelter, safety, love, air, health and to be part of something greater than oneself.

Wants: Everything that is not a need.

Home: Where you are with loved ones.

Satisfaction: A deep sense of accomplishment for a job well done.

Family: The people closest to you. The ones that would walk through a wall if you asked them to, and you would do the same for them.

Life: The eternal flame that connects all living beings.

Motivation: An internal drive that propels you in the direction you choose.

Responsibility: Taking care of something that is necessary.

Success: The ability to do what I want whenever I want to do it, while being part of something greater than myself.

You know what? I'm still tweaking this definition.

And now, my question for you is: what are your definitions of these words in your life?

Money	**Achievement**
Happiness	**Joy**
Work	**Needs**
Wants	**Home**
Satisfaction	**Family**
Life	**Motivation**
Responsibility	**Success**

CHAPTER 12

THE AGE OF HUMANITY

It is not enough to be industrious; so are the
ants. What are you industrious about?
—Henry David Thoreau

I'VE SPENT THE LAST THREE decades building my skills to make money by teaching others to make money, too. Like millions of others, I've honed my leadership ability and skills in the areas of strategy, execution and promotion.

Over the past five years, I've learned personally that kind of success makes for a very comfortable life but doesn't and didn't fulfill my need to feel part of something bigger than myself. I've certainly devoted a certain amount of time, energy and money toward charitable efforts, but now I don't think that's enough—not enough for myself and not enough for the world, either. I know there are many, many other "successful" people who also experience that same empty feeling.

I separate recent modern history, at least in the westernized parts of the world, into the Industrial Age and the Information Age. It seems to me that, during those two eras, a lot of society has been focused on building better lives for ourselves through capitalism. There's certainly been concern for less privileged or more troubled parts of the world, but our efforts to improve those areas have been relegated to philanthropy and non-profit organizations.

Conventional wisdom says that if enough of us donated money to the non-profit community they could take care of the world's problems while the rest of us concentrated on building capitalist societies. So, I could renounce my comfortable life and form or join a non-profit.

But that wouldn't be true to who I am. For better or worse, I'm a capitalist. I like making money and I'm good at it. I like working with others who are also successful capitalists. I enjoy helping successful people become even more successful.

What makes sense to me is for capitalists to refocus their skills, expertise and energy toward making the world a better place for everyone. Instead of just making more money and acquiring more things, I'd like to see people redefine success to mean making "enough" and working together to ensure that everyone has "enough."

I think there are ways to make a very comfortable living by solving our biggest social challenges, using skills we've already developed. The game of life might be survival of the fittest but, with the right efforts, everyone can survive—including those who might *not* be the fittest.

I call this The Age of Humanity.

Capitalism is the answer

I believe that capitalism—the original definition of capitalism as defined in John Mackay's book *Conscious Capitalism* is the key to social innovation and social change. Mackay says that Adam Smith defined capitalism as the creation of free cash flow and that over the past few decades, businesses and Wall Street have focused way too much on the financial return portion of capitalism.

Philanthropy and non-profit organizations, of course, have a role to play in making the world a better place for all humanity. But it's been my experience that entrepreneurship and capitalism are very powerful elements in society. The Age of Humanity creates and delivers a new awareness: it's time we harnessed that power to create a world in which everyone can live comfortably.

We need to ask the question:
What is enough?

Doing that will require some changes in our individual and collective mind-sets, but nothing so radical that it can't be accomplished. *Success Redefined* is the story of my own change of mindset, from one driven to be "successful" in the conventional sense—more money, more things, to a definition that includes purpose as well as a comfortable life. I think you'll see that my life is still comfortable, my family well-cared for, but I've gained a wider perspective on the world. If I can do it, so can you—if you're so inclined.

In the most successful cultures in history, the strong took care of the weak. In many of our modern societies, capitalists make up the ranks of the strong, but many have no interest in taking care of the weak. That has to change. We need to ask the question: "What is enough? When is it that we have enough and we can use our time, along with our skills and our money to affect the entire world around us?"

That's why I created **Success Redefined**, to help people realize their purpose and harness their collective power to effect change. Together, we can do so much more than any one of us can do alone. This is about sharing not only our wealth, but also our intellect and talents.

To understand my approach, I need to start with a few definitions:

Capitalism, according to Merriam-Webster, is "an economic system characterized by private or corporate ownership of capital goods, by investments that are determined by private decision as well as prices, production and the distribution of goods in a free market."

The *profit motive* is the desire of firms to maximize their profits—the money that exceeds the costs of material and production. In other words, the goal of the business is to make money.

Greed is the belief that any surplus generated by a business should flow into the pockets of the owner or shareholders. A greedy business owner will pursue only his or her own interests, seeking as much profit as possible, without regard to the needs of others.

It seems to me that, over the past few decades, the term "capitalism" has become synonymous with the word "greed." But they are not the same. It may be just my perspective, but I think a lot of the fault lies in our focus on our own financial well-being rather than focusing on everyone's well-being.

I don't believe in unlimited profits at all costs, with consideration only of the desire for more money. I do fully believe that the profit motive and capitalism are powerful tools to do well.

**Don't ask: *what* do you do;
instead ask: *who* are you?**

What I've observed over the past several years is that, despite all the passion and vision that fuel non-profit and philanthropic organizations, they can't by themselves bring about the lasting social change that our society needs. My conclusion is that the way to bring about social change is not through philanthropy alone. Pure, old-fashioned capitalism can be—should be—a significant part of the solution. The creation of free cash flow, sustainable free cash flow, invested into communities is the answer to changing lives for the better.

Building to give back

Building businesses on a foundation of discipline, paying competitive salaries and, yes, creating wealth for the owners, is the way to have a real impact on communities. There is a place, of course, for non-profit organizations. But they, too, will be most effective if they're built on those same strong, capitalist foundations.

Our culture in the US teaches us that we need to follow the path from high school to college to a job to moving up the corporate ladder, with each step bringing a sense of self-worth based on our title and things outside of ourselves. When I first meet people their initial question is "What do you do?" Why don't people ask, "Who are you?" I think it's a better question.

The challenge I see is to find a way for entrepreneurs and others to redefine success; to put their skills to use in a way that benefits society while steering away from the tendency to become very important, very busy people. In my own life, defining success to include being part of something bigger than myself has led me to the true joy of connecting with others who share that purpose.

There are various legal and financial structures to carry out that goal, which I'm not going to describe because this isn't a business book. But I do want to give just two examples, to show it can be done.

- Spark Ventures (www.SparkVentures.org) was created by Rich Johnson of Chicago. He visited an orphanage in Zambia. As he was leaving, Rich asked the orphanage's founder what he would like from Rich in the long-term. The answer was, help in making the organization self-sustaining. Rich's solution was to develop a chicken-farming model. The residents learn the business during their time at the farm, while selling the chickens produces revenue. The existing farm in Zambia is expected to become self-sustaining within five years and the organization is creating another chicken farm in Nicaragua.

- Solutions for Change (www.Solutionsfor Change.org) is a non-profit based in Vista, CA, that takes homeless families off the street. The founder, Chris Megison, has a vision that combines a for-profit venture with his non-profit. When Solutions for Change takes families off the street he has parents that need to go to work, so he puts them to work

on his aquaponics farm that produces
vegetables for the local school system.
The farm produces revenue that supports
the organization so the majority of donations
can go directly toward programs and not
overhead. This is how organizations in the
future need to think!

To me, those are appropriate and significant uses of philanthropy.

In addition to these amazing non-profits, Bill and Melinda Gates, along with Warren Buffett, have created the Giving Pledge for the world's billionaires. The objective is to help these families give away their fortunes in a constructive manner. There are numerous other organizations focused on redirecting capital to areas that need it, including the Robinhood Foundation and Social Venture Partners. The Robinhood Foundation, based in NYC, is focused on funding support organizations that are making a difference in the local area. Social Venture Partners, an organization founded in Seattle, uses funds from partners combined with their business acumen to invest in organizations making a difference in 40 cities around the world.

Investment Options

Most businesses need some seed money to get started and grow into sustainability. In this construct, non-profits get their investment from philanthropy as a gift, while the investor gets a tax deduction. On the other hand, for-profits use debt or equity for the investors as seed money.

We should be looking at all businesses as just that—businesses— some of which are not-for-profit and most are for-profit. The only difference is their tax status. All these organizations need to be built on a revenue model that provides value to their clients or customers, and return to their investors.

If you run a small business and your revenue model doesn't work, then you will eventually go out of business. If you run a non-profit and your revenue model doesn't work but you are great at fundraising, your business can go on forever. I don't believe that is a viable revenue model.

If we run all organizations on a "for-profit" model, we'll also reap the reward of developing generations of young people who will see the value of a socially conscious business. They will develop their own drive and skills, but they won't feel they have to flock to Wall Street in order to achieve a comfortable life.

CHAPTER 13

SUCCESS REDEFINED

Tell me, sir, what is a butterfly?

It's what you are meant to become. It flies with beautiful wings and joins the earth to heaven. It drinks only nectar from the flowers and carries the seeds of love from one flower to another. Without butterflies, the world would soon have few flowers.
—Trina Paulus

HOPE FOR THE FLOWERS IS the story of two caterpillars, Stripe and Yellow, who are searching for the meaning of life as a caterpillar. They find themselves at the base of a pillar of caterpillars and realize their purpose is to reach the sky.

They decide to climb to the top of the caterpillar pillar—the same goal as thousands of other caterpillars. Halfway up, Stripe and Yellow become disillusioned. Yellow feels especially bad about stepping on and climbing over all the other caterpillars striving to reach the sky.

The two descended. Yellow decided to follow the path toward becoming a butterfly, ate her leaves, spun a cocoon and emerged with wings. She flew effortlessly into the sky. Stripe, however, decided to climb the tower of caterpillars again, doing whatever was needed to reach the top.

This time, he succeeded. But again he was disappointed. He realized he wasn't in the sky at all. The only view he had was the sight of other caterpillars struggling to the top.

Stripe felt frozen. To be so high and not high at all! It only looked good from the bottom.

One day, Yellow circled the tower and Stripe caught sight of her. He realized he, too, yearned to become a butterfly.

There's nothing at the top
and it doesn't matter!
As he heard his own
message he realized how
he had misread the instinct
to get high.
To get to the top he
must fly, not climb.

Stripe climbed down, ate his leaves and spun a cocoon, while Yellow waited. When he emerged, they flew off together, content at last. In the end, Stripe realized his purpose was not to climb to the top of a caterpillar pillar, but to become a butterfly.

Hope for the Flowers, written by Trina Paulus was first published in 1972 and has been a favorite book of mine for years. I have recommended it to so many people and read it to our kids as often as I could. I believe there are so many parallels in our lives—for one, that climbing the corporate ladder did not lead me to happiness. Today I also see it as a fable that could define our values for decades to come.

Building for something better

Many of us have learned how to build great organizations with strong leadership, idea creation, strategy, execution and promotion. For those willing to take risks and put those skills and ideas to use, the end result has been financial gain. Some, but not all, of those people have found a way to redirect those capital rewards back into society.

That's why I created **Success Redefined**, to help people realize their purpose and harness their collective power to create social change. Together, we can do so much more than any one of us can do alone.

This is about sharing not only our wealth, but also our intellect and talents.

This may sound a little crazy, but I am focusing my efforts on people who already are "successful" in the conventional sense. It's my niche.

Here's my reasoning: If you are good at making money, you can monetize just about anything. Why not shift from making money for money's sake, to monetizing your reason for being? Those of us who are good at making money can reallocate our time and talents. We'll still live lives that are more than comfortable, but we will also experience the joy and connection that comes from helping others live comfortably, too.

I am on this planet to help "successful" people understand what they mean by that word. I'm here to help people who know very well how to make money, but are still searching for the purpose that will make them feel connected and significant.

I've developed a five-step methodology to help people rethink and redefine success. Here's a summary of the steps:

Definitions
Life Buckets
Core Values

Your Genius/Life's Work
Support System

You've already started the process, if you thought about and defined the 14 phrases I gave you in Chapter 11, *Failure to Define Success*. Did you find the definitions hard to pin down? Were the definitions you devised for yourself the same as the conventional understanding of the words? Are your definitions in sync with those of the important people in your life? I've found that assuming everyone understands words the same way I do to be a very bad assumption.

Allocating time and energy

The second step is recognizing how we spend our time and attention. If you actually take a week to map your activities and energy expenditures, you may be surprised to find your focus isn't where you thought it was—or intended it to be. Are you making time for what you say are your priorities in life, or are you too busy?

Genius, by my definition, is the thing you were put on this planet to do.

I've created a list of 10 "buckets" to analyze where I spend my time. Your list may be different, but here's mine:

1. Family
2. Friends
3. Faith
4. Health
5. Work
6. Fun/Recreation
7. Finance
8. Education
9. Spirituality
10. Self-Actualization through Purpose

The third step is articulating core values. My work at this point is to align everything in my life according to my values. Most of us have several values that we try to honor. One of mine is to spend my energy with people who are self-aware, who are living a life of purpose, and who can get things done. I want to make intentional choices based on values that I share with the people around me.

Up until a few years ago, I didn't stop to think if my career was my "life's work," or whether it reflected my genius. It was my career and it supported my family. But in the process of exploring all the issues

I've written about, I took another look at the phrase "life's work" and I redefined it. I think now that my work is more solidly built on a foundation of my *genius*.

By "genius," I don't mean IQ or any other measure of intelligence. Genius, by my definition, is the thing you were put on this planet to do. You can wake up each morning and just be you. The ideal is to combine your genius and your life's work to produce sufficient income to live a comfortable, productive life. That's my ultimate destination.

Don't hurry, enjoy the trip!

As I wrote earlier, self-examination is an on-going process. You may not be able to take advantage of your particular genius in your current profession— yet. So you find some other way to live your purpose. Who knows? You may discover a way to monetize that purpose. Or you may, in the process of reassessment, discover an even higher purpose.

The fifth step, and the key to success, is creating a support system. It starts with a plan and people to help you toward your destination. The plan may change, but the same people may not ride along for the entire journey. In my own life, my business partner for 19 years and I learned a lot of valuable lessons together. We supported and complemented one another. But our roads have parted. That doesn't devalue what we experienced together. Remember, reaching your destination isn't a day trip—it's a lifetime journey, it's a marathon.

Finally, to be successful, both in the conventional sense and in my more intentional, purpose-filled version, there are five key skills required to build businesses. It doesn't matter whether these businesses are for-profit or not-for-profit, the skills are required for both. These skills are:

- Leadership
- Ideation
- Strategy
- Execution
- Promotion

I spent most of my professional life climbing the ladder of success. Like Stripe, I made it to the top, but found the view uninspiring, even depressing. I looked for fulfillment in a number of different directions, including self-improvement and various charitable contributions. But until I got clarity on who I am, what I'm good at and what I care about, the choices I made were pretty unintentional.

So the challenge I see is to find a way for entrepreneurs and others to redefine success, to put those five key skills to use in a way that benefits society while steering away from the tendency to become very important, very busy people.

In my own life, defining success to include being part of something bigger than myself has led me to the true joy of connecting with others who share that purpose. My connections are deeper because they are built on a purpose level, not a surface level.

Not to get into the confusing use of business jargon—you know, what's a goal, what's a strategy, what's a tactic—but I do see a difference between my mission and my purpose.

My *mission* is to build a support system to help people that have found financial and business success be successful in using those same business skills to create a better world. I'm not here to define your purpose—you have to do that yourself.

My *purpose* is to connect people who have those skills to one another and help them take on this journey with that support team. It's an ability that not everyone has, but which I have in abundance.

I'm a "connector," both on an individual and organizational level. I hope this book, by example, inspires you to reach out and find your tribe—connect with other like-minded and like-hearted people.

You don't have to be a billionaire like Bill and Melinda Gates and Warren Buffett to help and support others. Who is doing the same thing that they are with the Giving Pledge concept for the millions of people of wealth that are not billionaires? Do you have to be a billionaire to give away moneys? I don't think so.

We have so much pent-up desire to have deep conversations about who we know we can be. There just aren't enough opportunities to have these conversations. If I can help make that change happen, if I can connect a worthy organization with people or other organizations that help them get their jobs—whatever that job is—done, then I've served my purpose.

CHAPTER 14

AFTERWORD

Let's redefine success together, make the world
a better place and begin to feel human again.
—Larry Kesslin

SUCCESS REDEFINED IS MY BREADCRUMB out in the world looking to find my tribe, those other business leaders who want to use their business acumen to create a better world.

If you are successful based on the conventional definition of success, if you are very important and very busy, but still feel there is something meaningful missing; or you are already on the purpose journey and want to share ideas with other like-minded and like-hearted professionals, I'd love to hear from you.

It's been my experience that overcoming fear, reaching out and expressing myself and taking the road filled with more meaning is extremely rewarding. My hope is that my story will give you some inspiration and ideas to rewrite your own life story around a purpose that brings you deeper connections and an abiding sense of joy. Let's redefine success together, make the world a better place and begin to feel human again.

Finally, I am a work in progress. I promise you that, if you meet me on the street or talk with me at some future date, my thoughts and ideas will have evolved again.

To a life well lived—with purpose,
deep connections and joy!

ABOUT THE AUTHOR

Larry Kesslin is an entrepreneur, speaker, author, consultant and coach who lives in Carlsbad, CA with his wife, Ilise, and their two children, 15 year old daughter Drew and 13-year-old son Noah. Larry started his career with Westinghouse and then spent 5 years with GE before venturing out on his own in 1993.

He is the coauthor of *BreakPoints* that reveals hidden pitfalls and obstacles that can easily tarnish or destroy a business.

Larry has spent the past two decades focused on making money and now he is totally focused on using his success skills to leave this planet infinitely better than he found it. Larry has worked hard to learn to be present and now wants to teach others how to live their purpose and feel more complete in their lives.

Contact him at:

www.LarryKesslin.com

Larry@LarryKesslin.com

LinkedIn:
https://www.linkedin.com/in/larrykesslin

WORKING WITH LARRY KESSLIN

Larry is very focused on helping people that want to make a difference in the world. If you are looking to leave a legacy that uses your business acumen, or the results of your business skills, then he is here to serve you. As a successful person we all want to see results from our actions. Working on the right projects that can actually accomplish our goals is critical to our long-term satisfaction from our giving efforts. Being of service is the most selfish act we can do, but giving of self to projects that have very little future can cause some frustration.

Larry works with clients one-on-one globally and in peer groups in San Diego. His firm, Success Redefined, is all about helping those drawn to this cause to find each other. Many might feel like needles in a haystack. Larry is a magnet that pulls all the individual needles out and introduces them to each other. In the end, it's all about evolving our culture from "Me" to "We"!

CPSIA information can be obtained
at www.ICGtesting.com
Printed in the USA
FSOW03n0135151215
14219FS